Stories From The Bush

To order additional copies of this book, contact:
Xlibris
1-800-455-039
www.xlibris.com.au
Orders@Xlibris.com.au

AS IT WAS

Water

Mother and friend

Stone for a new home

Grandfather and Uncles

CONTENTS

"Dad", came the voice of my brother, muffled and sleepy, "why do you cook an extra chop for breakfast?". And our father, who'd lived through the depression, replied, "It's for the lady on a white horse".

Boundary rider's hut

Saltbush plains

THE LADY ON A WHITE HORSE

Many were they in the depression

Forced to live away from home

A roof of a hut and meat ration

They were better than on the roam

Long days on the saltbush plain

Burning heat while he worked.

The horse's swish of tail and mane

Where only loneliness lurked

The nights were long and cold

Of friends and family he dreamt.

And the girl he wanted to hold,

The last letter she had sent

The lazy night wind lulled

Him finally to sleep

All life's desires dulled

He slumbered ever deep.

He heard her as dawn was breaking

Calling for some rations for her ride,

A vision of a white horse, as he was waking

Then it melted and died.

He could hear her call so softly

Through the mist in the early light

Her white horse shone so brightly

Her long hair a marvellous sight.

"And so", said my Dad, "Next time I'll have some rations for her"

****

When my Aunt had the job of babysitting me, she took me along all the back roads and stockroutes . We drove in her old Oakland and I remember stopping to chat to a drover as he sat in his horse and trap reading the paper, and letting his sheep graze the' long paddock'. My Aunt loved the station country and the people in it.

Many years later I drove a mob along that same route.

Nearly home

Stock route

See the red dust rising

RED DUST (BILLY)

Set the gates; check the waters

Everyone be near

See the red dust rising

The mob is nearly here.

The mob streamed before me

Then at a tree the leaders baulked.

What disturbed them I could not see,

But this was where Billy walked

I saw him in a child's haze

A horse-drawn cart he drove,

The long paddock his to graze

The mob of the whiskery old cove

He had driven many mobs

From stations way up north

Now there were no more droving jobs

He just plied the road back and forth

Up to the front my dog I sent

To get them moving along

Not wanting to know what I meant

She acted as though she was wrong

I really think Billy scolded her,

Only his own dog could do the part.

But how could a ghost make all waver

And fear the man in the cart?

The cold wind cut across the plain,

A relief from the heat for a while.

The sheep moved easily making gain;

Through the home gate they'd soon file.

They said "did you have trouble on the way

Near where that one tree stands?.

An old drover died there one day

With his dog, and reins in his hands"

****

Old shearing sheds have a mystical feel about them. Somehow you can hear and see the men still,

With the ever thumping engine and the flap of belts and whirring of the wheels that turned the head and downpiece.

Blade early 1900s

Shearers

Wheels

Shearing young ram

THE GHOST ON THE 4TH STAND

Off with the belly, clean up the crutch

Push up through the neck and round the shoulder too

Down on your knee, the long blow's an easy touch

Tidy round the tail, and that's all you've got to do

Hear the engine as it builds up its thumps.

Shears are warmed and then they sing.

Doors are swinging as they drag out their lumps.

The orchestra is playing as all shears ring.

Listen to the running along the board

Woolpress clicking...banging of the broom

All's such a race until they pull their cord

Handpieces down and then calm in the room.

I hear their laughter; I feel their pain

I smell the sweat and lanolin in the shed

I know they're tired but they'll be back again

There's money they've tallied already in their head

I'm the ghost on the 4th stand; I set the pace.

I've got them worried as they feel someone's there.

I can see them checking; puzzlement on their face

As they push harder, admit they wouldn't dare

I hear them talking as they wipe their brow

"Believe old Mick in the 50's could turn out a few.

They say he's in the rest home; quite a cripple now".

But I am there, on the 4th stand . I'm shearing with you.

****

They met him on the station in the Top End.

Cutting practice

Helicopter and horses for muster

Stragglers

JIMMY

Jimmy was a ringer

Head stockman he became

At the Top End he did linger

A horse and cattleman of fame

The ringer on the rails

He coaxed into the yard

The ringer she was pretty

And she took him off his guard

The stirry mob they caught him

And brought him to the ground

Through the dust his view was dim

But her hero she had found

But Jimmy had a dream

Chopper to muster cattle

Leave horses to the mustering team

While skies he strove to battle.

Scrub was thick, cows hard to find.

Jimmy searched too low.

In one swift move his life he'd signed

'Way to where the good men go

A mother's softly crying.

A father a son he's lost.

And a pretty ringer's sighing

For what the chopper cost.

Jimmy, wont you please come home?

Jimmy, the cattle are on the roam.

Jimmy, the ringers are all near.

So bring the chopper here.

(We're still waiting here.)

****

It seems I've had many times in hospital. The loneliness and trepidation at night when kept awake with pain makes you alert to other movements in the building.

A QUIET SHADOW

Just a quiet shadow
Melting in the dark room

Late at night she came
So softly all alone

Hardly even breathing
She slipped beneath the sheet

But then there was such sobbing
As can only come from the soul

Shaking silhouette against the wall
Curled in innocence in her bed

She whispered in her mobile
Then settled so quietly

When all was still before day broke

He came and took her away

Two dark figures floating by

Two lovers so young and sad

From where did they come

And where did they go?

****

Returning to the old home and back to sheep work meant going to see the sheep sell at the market.

It had been so long ago and some faces were vaguely familiar.

As it was

Present day sale Mid-north S.A.

ADONIS

This was where we all hung out.

Adonis, the man above the rest.

Admired and sought by all about

To hear and see; he was the best.

They all gathered round the pen

Where the auctioneer reigned

Buyers, sellers, all keen men

Eager to see what each bid gained

"What's your bid, what's your bid

Give this lot a start.

You must buy, he must rid

Money or sheep must part"

Then they moved as one great mob

Following the man on the board

Banter and quick wit was the job

Rising bids, then the final chord.

Old, young men and women did follow

Studying each pen of dusty sheep

Trucking and yarding had some hollow

But all were for a buyer to keep.

All was quiet when the last pen sold

Then men's rumbling voices again

On prices and stories untold

This was the world of old sheep men

Trucks roar as to ramps they back

Whistle and shouts to dogs and sheep

Busy racing laneways pack

With endless lines of those to keep

Amongst the crowd as it milled around

Some bloke in a wheel chair

With hands weathered and browned

Looked up, and then; I saw him there.

Was it him, the Adonis of the north

The young auctioneer, adored by all?

He, who could only have gone forth.

So long ago: let it be; hear the auctioneer's call.

****

In a place where the Merino sheep ruled for many generations, the shadows and echoes in the hills remind them of their past.

Shadows on the Hill

Here's where the future lies

SHADOWS ON THE HILL

See the whispy dust blowing up the gum-lined track.

Hear the dry grass whisper as it swirls round and back.

With the sky in purple array, angry clouds race by

Threatening storms today, to break the mid north's dry.

Hear the mounting noise now

Men shedding the sheep

Barking dogs make such a row

Dry wool they want to keep

How many years has this been.

Sheep the only way.

A future had been seen

By those before today

Smell the rain on dry red earth.

See wet rocks above.

Hear the creeks at last give birth.

Feel with the place you love.

There's a home set in the hillside

Above the valley below,

Where love and warmth abide

And future footsteps go

There's shadows on the hill.

Listen to their echoing cries.

They are calling softly still.

Here's where your future lies.

****

Memory

There comes a time when you know it's time to quit. It's hard but you know it. You're too slow or can't handle your bike or horse the same, and when you fall, the bones hurt for too long, if they mend at all.. The rocks you see are probably sheep, and the dogs can't hear your feeble yell.

Sheep coming down hill

Author, dog, and bike

Mustering before motor bikes

HIS LAST MUSTER

"Go higher,higher

Send the dogs higher

Higher, higher

Or they'll get away

Higher,higher

Go a bit higher

Or you'll end up with no sheep today"

The old man sat in his rocking chair

As his grandfather did before.

He watches as the sheep downward tear

And the cunning ones escaping he saw

He knew every rock and places they ran

Knew how to find them and where.

By horse or by bike as good as any man.

Now watching was more than he could bear

The mountains and rock rising above him

As down to the yard the sheep streamed.

Every moment was relived by the old man

And the chair rocked harder it seemed

Push up to the yards and leave them.

Down to the house; all bikes away.

Tie up the dogs and feed them...

But grandpa has had his last muster today

****

It was a ritual. Go see grandma.

James and Charlotte

DON'T CRY, GRANDMA

Up the dark passage two little girls crept
To a light from a door.
There they knew their grandmother slept
Never to rise any more.

In the dark room their grandmother lay
Just a window for light.
'Shh,or you'll frighten my friends away
Who make my poor life bright"

"My world is just the little I see
And all that I'm able to hear.
Go to the window and there my friends will be.
Be quiet and they'll stay near."

On tiptoe they stretched to the sill
Only a vine could they see
Far behind was the woolshed set on the hill
But grandmother's friends they could not see.

"See, she's fluttering round the nest
There hiding deep in the vine.
If you listen, their cheeps you'll hear best
As they cry out to dine"

"Now my dears, my needle I must take.
You mustn't hear me cry."
Outside they waited for grandmother to make
The cries they remember her by

Don't cry grandma.
The little birds might hear you.
Don't cry grandma.
They'll fly away if you do

Up the dark passage two little girls race
Into a cold and lonely room.
Evening shadows drifted through the lace
But grandmother's friends had left too.

Don't cry grandma
Your friends might hear you
Don't cry grandma.
They've flown away with you too.

****

Topical

There are so many tragedies. The world news tells us all. Are we cacooned enough 'down under'.?

How would we handle such awful things, and yet...

HOW CAN WE KNOW THEIR PAIN

How can we known their pain

With the loss of those who died

Young ones never to return again

Homes forever gone in the great slide

But I can hear their cries,

I can see them in the rubble,

How can they go on with their lives?

It all seems so much fruitless trouble.

But there will always be a Sichuan.

Another horror, another blow.

Our world tests each man.

We can hope we'll never know .

But hear the whisper of the gums

And magpies warble in the morn.

Feel the heat of summer as it comes,

Always for us a new day is born

****

Love

Seems to rule our lives, from our mother's love to the challenging sort.

LOVE , LOVE , LOVE.....

Love, love love, what an illusion
Love, love love, why's there such confusion?

How does it happen, where does it go?
One minute all roses, next thing it's woe.
Why does it tease some and let others go?
Why such delusion to fool poor hearts so?

How does it give its victims such bloom?
How does it bring its magic with the moon?
Why does it cast its net in a room
Eager to send two people to their doom

How does it weaken even the strongest men?
How does it give strength to little women?
Every time it bites there's left a scar again
So, love, love, love are you a good omen?

Love, love, love what an illusion
Love, love, love why's there such confusion?

****

Julia in window

LOOK FOR THE LIGHT

My mother always told me

When in the dark I'd cry

Through the window you'll see dear

There's a light in the sky.

While there is a light near

You can see where you go.

Nothing can hurt dear

Or take you too low.

When we're sad and heart-broken

And there's nothing left right

The sweet words that were spoken

Tell me to look for the light.

Those who walk with me

Who fear the dark night

Their mother didn't set free

To look for the light.

Look for the light, dear, there's always a light dear....

****

THICK GLASS WALLS

Thick glass walls are mocking me

Letting me see what you do

Thick glass walls are blocking me

Locking me away from you

They all love to be around you

I can see you acting so cool

Drinking,dancing and flirting too

Glass walls make me a fool.

How come you don't see me crying?

Longing to be just with you.

Why do I keep on pining?

When glass walls wont let me through?

They say as we get older

And thinner becomes the glass,

And when my love turns colder,

Glass walls will let me pass.

No thick glass walls now to mock me

Thick glass walls won't block me

No thick glass walls to lock me

Away from the one who loves me.

****

Our youngest daughter' wedding...

TOGETHER

Walk, talk together

Strength is built on love.

When the bond you sever,

The world is far above.

When we walked together

When we were young and bold

The world was ours forever

Ours to take and mould.

When we talked together

When we thought as one

The world was ours to better

Ours to make and run.

Feel those strong warm hands.

Hear that manly tone.

The world is ours forever.

Ours never to take alone.

Feel the softness of her skin.

See her gentle way.

The world is ours forever.

Ours to share each day .

Walk, talk together.... strength is built on love.

****

Phillips River

YOUTH REMEMBERED

Like the running brook is your love

Which in the winter roars

And when there' s no clouds up above

Like placid pools will it pause.

Or will it flow with endless waves

Crashing on the shore

Till your love she craves

You ebb and there's no more.

Hear the brook, as it charms

Feel the sea with its mist so fresh

Frolic with love that only harms

If love and soul enmesh.

Youth and love together roam

Lightly to be taken

The senses fly and have no home

In time all will awaken.

Let me fly, let me return

And let me relive my youth.

Let me again of freedom learn

Away from life's eternal truth

****

Ready to leave the nest

Grandchildren

The oldest grandchildren

Music, family passion

WILL THEY COME?

As the red clouds sink on the horizon

And day is gone rapidly

There's love still there awaiting

Sure as rivers run to the sea.

Whispy hair and sad eyes

Adorn the crinkled face

She can hear the happy cries

Of children as they play.

She sees their tiny fingers

Feels their satin cheeks

Knows their teenage whispers

Her memories are so clear.

The house drowns in it's silence

The passage leads nowhere

Once spreading such a warm sense

Now a house so cold and bare

Knobby hands keep fingering

Photos on the wall.

Hungry arms are lingering

Ready to embrace them all.

But they know not what they do

Those cherished pride and joys

Who swelled the heart and pained it too

No longer girls and boys.

Edging the farmland plains

Tomorrow just a haze.

Today's clear blue mountains

Echo life's elusive ways

Soon a light shines brightly

Quietness surrounds the home.

Gum trees stir but softly,

And a mother still waits alone

****

Written as a waltz; now shortened.

COME BACK, COME BACK, MY LOVE.

I thought our love was for our life

Never to be taken away

How could it go before we knew

And leave us with no say.?

We'll never share the dreams we had

Our lives together are done

But I will live each day for you

Until my life is run

Come back, come back come back my love

Come back . come back to me.

Although our love was for our life

You have been taken from me.

****

New World

Sometimes you have to move on. The beautiful hills must be left behind. A mist that comes and floats around the hills is like a curtain being drawn, shutting away the hills and creeks of home, as it is time to leave and start a new life.

Mist on the Hills

Gateway to Home

Snow on the hills

THE CURTAIN

I feel the icy sleet

On rocky ridges high

Where all the mountains meet

And lonely sheaoks sigh

In every running creek

I hear your happy song

Your craggy face I seek

Etched in rocks so proud and strong

Swiftly rolling down the rocky hill

Blotting out sun and sky

The mist keeps on tumbling till

Reaching where the valley lies

Dark, cold and oh so still,

Mystery surrounds the range

As the curtain draws on every hill

Frightening is the change.

Fluffy white mist is falling

Swiftly covering rocks and trees

Lost little lambs are calling

In the mountain's misty seas

It's time to leave it all behind

Leave the womb in clouded mist.

Another world there is to find

If such a place exists.

The curtain now is drawn

On what is left today

The old world from me is torn

Don't look back. I'm on my way

****

Leaving their small home farms in the eastern states of Australia, to take up 'new land 'in far off Western Australia, they were modern day pioneers. When they return to their old homes, the Nullarbor calls them back to W.A. But did they miss family and friends and the home left behind?

Shed

The new land farmer is no more

DO THEY SIGH

A new world they would create

So far from the family farm

They were so young and couldn't wait

Farewelling in saddened calm.

Hear the wind as it cuts across

And through the gaps in the iron

Put another rug around the cot

Another stump on the old No. 1.

Do they sigh for what's left behind

Or do they look far ahead?

Do they cry for the ties that bind

Or ambition's path do they tread?

See the snake as the toddler plays

Near the bags of super on the ground.

It's not easy with children to raise

And no proper comforts around.

See the dust and smoke down there

Where he clears and rakes the new land.

He doesn't see the acres so bare

Only pasture and green on the sand

When they go with weathered heart,

Their old home is not the same.

Too many days since their depart.

No warm voices call their name

Beckoning them is the Nullarbor.

Her inviting plain of freedom calls.

The new land farmer is no more.

His home in the west has no walls.

They don't sigh for what's left behind

For they are now far ahead.

They don't cry for the ties that bind

For ambition's path did they tread

****

New sandplain land was covered with various low scrub trees. The blue mallee tree is an attractive low tree which loads up with blossom. There's a story that when it blossoms heavily, there will be a good season following. However, whether it is good enough to bring the struggling farmer home from work and money elsewhere, to carry on with his 'block', is debatable...

Blue Mallee in flower

BLUE MALLEE

When the blue mallee flowers again, call me

When it's blossoms drip honey, call me

I know then that there will be rain

So when flowers are on the mallee, call me.

I've waited too long for good seasons

The blowing sand dried all my tears

You've given me all the reasons

For drought and wasted years.

So now I've gone and the sky is blue.

No rain to covet or dust to hate.

Just a lonely path and nothing to do,

But wonder whether it's too late.

The mines are luring me away.

They give me money for my toil.

There's just nothing every day

To replace the ache for my own soil.

I see the blue mallee in the night

When the lights make the blue leaves glow

A city of irredescent light

In the heath scrub couched below.

Eucalyptus scent lingers in me

It reigns above the mining smells

Calling for flowers on the blue mallee

Until in grief my lonely heart swells

Calling for the rains, the blue mallee knows

Ahead it tells what season is in store

With rain in the west or dry wind blows

Call me when it flowers, and I'll wait no more.

Oh, to be young again........ after a hot day, and all chores finished, unhitch the reins from the branch and take a wild ride up the lane in the moonlight.....

Lane

Dad and brother after the bull dozer

THE CHALLENGE

So long since the branch held

The reins of a restless horse

The York gum still stands there

But the branch has run its course.

It was springy and so high

Challenge to the pulling mare.

Now rotten on the ground and dry,

Its spring is beyond repair.

"But the memories awaken

Of you pulling as you paced.

With all cares forsaken

In the moonlight as we raced.

Down the lane your hoofs pound

Echoing in the balmy night.

Mottled carpet on the ground;

Jam tree canopy sifting light.

Smell the sweat, feel the strength

Of rippling muscle beneath.

As we run the lane's length

I can barely breath."

An old lady can be seen

Shuffling around near that tree.

She lived here as a teen

When she was young and free.

When that branch was young

When challenge could be held

When on it could be hung

The reins that made her world.

****

His sharp call early in the morning, wakened me. A lone bird seemed to be bringing a message. The river had been low for so long..... had he come from the Grampians, to the Glenelg River?

THE RIVER BELLBIRD

Will it flow,will it flow, will the river flow again

Does he know, does he know, it's coming?

Hear the bell, hear the bell, does the bellbird tell us when

The water will soon be running.?

The screeching of the white cockatoos

In the flood gums down below,

Echoes loudly through the gully

Where the river used to flow.

Wakes the little town so early

On this bright and sunny morn.

While the bell bird has sung his lone song

Since the break of dawn

Do they call for the river to flow.

So long since its been in flood.

The bellbird up so early,does he know,

The river'll soon be more than mud?

Far from the forest has he flown

In the distant misty mountains

Did a stormy wind have him blown

As the river trickled with the rains?

Will it flow, will it flow, will the river flow again?

Does he know, does he know, it's coming?

Hear the bell, hear the bell, does the bellbird tell us when

The water will soon be coming?

****

Even the most dedicated farmer can be glad to rest up. Takes a while to realise that it is possible to get up in the morning, and smell the roses,

Air Seeder

TAKE ME BACK---BUT DON'T

Take me back, take me back, but don't

Take me back, take me back, but don't

I've seen it all before

I don't want any more

Please just take me back

Please take me back to where I yearn

Where the air is fresh and does smell so good

When seeding time comes round once again

I'd be back there on the tractor if I could

But I don't want to mend a fault

I don't want the skun knuckles any more

I don't want to mend, weld or check any bolt

Or find out what wires of lines have worn raw.

I hear the cows way down the back

The sheep are calling to their baby lambs

But I don't want another tousle with the pack

Or handle flyblown ewes or cranky rams.

With budgets, bankers and dead sheep

Bogged tractors and the paddocks of windblown sand.

Never knowing what you can expect to reap

We all still do have that feeling for the land.

Take me back, take me back, but don't

Take me back, take me back, but don't

I've seen it all before

I don't want any more

Please just take me back.

****

Dogs

You can have dogs without sheep. Some people have sheep without dogs. Of course, I only mean DOGS. So dogs and no sheep seems a waste of time, and sheep and no dogs can definitely be a waste of time. At the same time I think dogs consider it's more fun to waste time, just for fun. You know what I mean......just cut one off the mob, or maybe chase after a lamb, or especially if there's a 'roo, just give the boss some practice with his lungs and language. But, do you know, the toughest of blokes shed a tear when something bad happens to HIS dog. The next story is of a dog losing his mate.

Henry patting dog

THE DOG'S MATE

Don't cry for me my young mate

As we linger and say goodbye

Let me go through that last gate

We've had such fun you and I

For I've some place to go

Where the utes are not too high

Where I can nip cows down low

And sheep I can make fly

Where the flies and birds wont tease

And roos and emus wont turn

There's a place that has no fleas

And bones and meat to burn

Where whispering trees tell their secrets

And moonlight nights show their ghost

There's a place for all man's pets

But you've been the greatest host

Your gentle whistle I hear

My tail has lost its wag

I try to lick that hand so dear

My eyes are closing, and sag,

Goodbye my young mate.

****

My dog was hyperactive. None of the other dogs liked her, and wherever she was, there was trouble. So returning home from the shearing and lots of sheep work, over a few weeks, they just wanted to lie in the back of the twin cab and dream of every ewe they'd had to straighten out and all the exciting bones they'd discovered on the old place. But my dog...no.... she still had lots of energy. I could have still sent her round a mob getting away on the side of the steep hills. So before there was a blood bath, we put her in the trailer behind, where she promptly made faces at the others in the front, while running around incessantly the perimeter of the trailer. She must have leant a bit too far through the rails while sneering at the others, and as it came daylight, we could see she wasn't there.

young dog in sheepyards

Nullarbor sunset

50

LITTLE DOG LOST

Head West little dog, and you can't go wrong

Past the saltbush, mulga and mallee.

When you smell the salmon gums as you trot along,

You'll know in a few days you'll be home to me.

The Nullarbor is cold at night.

The dingoes roam around.

She found shelter in the closing light,

At the water tanks where she was found

What long and lonely days

Running on the endless plain.

Through the roadside grassy maze,

Ignoring her cuts and pain.

She'd been there at the water tank

A couple of days ago.

She skirted round before she sank

And lapped the tap pool low

It's a long time to be on your own

Nobody to say 'way back'

No chain at night, no mates, no bone

No lights or noise from the shack

Trot, trot, trot, try to keep a guard

Keep nose close to the ground

All mixed smells making it so hard

Why isn't my boss around?

Head west little dog, and you can't go wrong

Past the saltbush, mulga and mallee

When you smell the salmon gums as you trot along

In a few days you'll be home to me.

****

It was Christmas. So many years ago, when the hospital was still in army style, just curtains between each patient and of course, no such thing as airconditioning. Hot weather meant open French doors out into a quadrangle. My father was extremely ill with cancer, as was most of the other men in the ward.

My mother tackled the long drive in the heat to visit my father, bringing with her a grandchild, who was their pride and joy.

The next story/poem, tells the story of a little boy, but, even though it was their grandchild, fortunately, he was not a sick little boy.

Conducting

AND A LITTLE BOY SHALL LEAD THEM

Around the quadrangle

Lit by candle glow

Bedridden men

Lay sad and low

Like angels the voices

Of the nurses rung

Carols for those who

To life clung

From the darkness

Marched a very little chap

Standing before the choir

In his cap

Waving thin arms

Conducting he led

Then raised his cap

Bare was his head

Such a white face

Lit by candlelight

A sick little boy

led the night

Husky voices crept

In a crescendo

Beds moved with life

At last let flow

And a little boy shall lead them

To heartfelt joy and hope.

To take each piece of life

Christmas is no time to mope.

Merry, merry, merry Christmas.

May there be many more.

Christ was born this day,

Giving us much to live for.

****

Rupara stars

Author

Rosalie Hill, has spent most of her life in Western Australia, helping her parents and then her husband develop new land to increase the family's business operations.

The family farm in South Australia was set amongst the hills in the mid-north, and held many fond memories of grandparents and life in the sheep country.

After a short working holiday around Australia, being employed as a telephonist, pay clerk and a teacher's college student, her career path then followed her husband's.

Having been educated at an exclusive girl's college did not equip her for the basics of the 'new land farmer's' wife, but with five children to raise and educate, tractors and rakes to drive, and making a home in the end of a machinery shed, she was in the company of many others doing the same.

Always it has been the love of the land that has motivated her life and ambitions.

Author and husband

AKNOWLEDGEMENTS

Clive Palmer, photography, JAMESTOWN S.A.

Historical Society, JAMESTOWN S.A.

Thank you for saleyard photos.

Peter Norville,

Thank you for old shearing shed photo, overhead gear.

David Marland Photography,
Thank you for photos in mid-north S.A.

Liveringa Station. Jed O'brien.
Thank you for photo of helicopter mustering

Patricia Flynn. Dan

Thank you for being the patient daughter and helping

With my latest project

Len, thank you for various photos taken on the road

Julianne, thank you for family photos

Various family members, thank you for acting as models.

"AUSSIE" TERMS

An understanding of the 'Aussie' terms .

Stumps, refers to the mallee tree roots which have been pulled out with the clearing of the new land . When dried, after a year or more, burn hot and quickly in the Metters wood cooking stove . No. 1. refers to the smallest version of stove. Super, which came in bags before bulk delivery, refers to fertiliser. Clearing and raking refers to the necessary activities to have the ground ready for farming. It takes a few seasons before it can be considered arable, farming land. 'Gaps in the iron'. Most new land farmers had little money, and the home for many years, consisted of a galvanised iron shed. 'Sand'. Most new land developed was a sandplain, as red soil country had been farmed much earlier.

The pioneering meant all people were equal and there were no social barriers or walls as in the earlier settlements of Australia, thus, "his home in the west has no walls".. Also there were many opportunities for any expansion or ambition in the West.

Cutting, a sport and as a means of separating an animal from the main mob.

Stragglers, also a term used to describe the stock found after the main muster .

****